Living Daily in the Word

Devotions by the
Ladies of
Calvary Chapel Living Word

Revelation 22:17

"And the Spirit and the bride say, "Come!"
And let him who hears say, "Come!"
And let him who thirsts come.
Whoever desires, let him take the water of life freely".

Living Daily in the Word
Calvary Chapel Living Word
Irvine, CA

Copyright 2013 - Living Word
Living Word Publishers

Printed in the United States of America.

ISBN-978-1-304-57679-8

Contents

Acknowledgments

We first and foremost want to thank our Lord Jesus Christ, "for in Him we live and move and have our being" (Acts 17:28). We would like to thank Pastor Jon Miller for the beautiful cover illustration. We are so appreciative of Nancy Tumbas, Jan Arant and Candy Ohanian for their commitment to editing this book. Thank you to Emil Jaksa for his patience and timing at the photo shoot, you had an eye for catching us beautifully! We want to thank our Pastor, Terry Walker, for being so faithful in teaching us God's Word and being a loving shepherd to us. We thank the congregation at Calvary Chapel Living Word for their faithfulness to God's Word: "And let us consider one another in order to stir up love and good works, not forsaking the assembling of ourselves together, as is the manner of some, but exhorting one another, and so much the more as you see the Day approaching" (Hebrews 10:24-25).

We are eternally grateful to the Lord for Pastor Chuck Smith, who just went home to heaven this last month. He was a mentor to us all. "I have fought the good fight, I have finished the race, I have kept the faith" (2 Timothy 4:7).

We thank the Lord for you, the reader. May the real Author speak to you.

Preface

These devotions have been composed by some of the ladies and teenage girls from Calvary Chapel Living Word in Irvine, California. They have poured out their hearts, sharing personal experiences of God's faithfulness. These devotions will bless and edify as they are all inspired by the Word of God. Their love for Jesus is evident as you read what they have penned. We have also included a few poems that will encourage your heart. Some of our favorite devotions by Oswald Chambers, Anne Graham Lotz and quotes by Amy Carmichael are included in the book. Grab a cup of coffee, relax & enjoy a "spiritual spa day" and see how the Lord desires to speak to you through God's Word and these writings.

Our prayer for you is that your faith will be increased as you seek Him with all of your heart.

"For all the promises of God in Him are Yes, and in Him Amen, to the glory of God through us" (II Cor. 1:20).

"But without faith it is impossible to please Him, for he who comes to God must believe that He is, and that He is a rewarder of those who diligently seek Him." (Hebrews 11:6).

May you be blessed!

Only by His grace,

Sheila Walker, Pastor's Wife/Women's Ministry

" I have no greater joy than to hear that my children walk in truth"
(3 John 1:4).

One of my greatest treasures rests on the shelf in my husband's office at church. It is a framed picture of each of our three children when they were dedicated to the Lord as infants, and a picture next to it of them making the choice to be baptized into our Lord Jesus Christ. I truly have no greater joy than to hear my children walk in the Truth. I praise God that each of their spouse's know and serve the Lord, they are my kids now, too, whom I love dearly.

This leads me to our granddaughter, Kate. How she teaches me about God's love on a regular basis, she is chock-full of ways to minister to Mimi. She has a great sense of humor that tickles me, even at her young age! We have so much fun together. She loves life and it shows! I'm sure God gives us grandchildren to have them demonstrate things to us which we have forgotten! I'm reminded of the verse in 2 Timothy 1:5: "...when I call to remembrance the genuine faith that is in you, which dwelt first in your grandmother Lois and your mother Eunice, and I am persuaded is in you also." It is an awesome responsibility. Kate is blessed to have a godly mother and father. I have chosen to be a godly grandmother that will help her parents point her to the Lord.

I want her to see in me that "genuine faith". I want to live out with her what I pray I did for our own children in Deuteronomy 6: "And these words which I command you today shall be in your heart. You shall teach them diligently to your (grand) children, and shall talk of them when you sit in your house, when you walk by the way, when you lie down, and when you rise up." Kate and I 'discuss' what a beautiful ocean God made, what a sense of humor God has in some funny looking fish He created...it's an ongoing conversation.

Let's be sure to pray daily for our children and grandchildren to walk strong in the Lord and the power of His might. What better gift can we give them?

-Sheila Walker

"He will cover you with his feathers. He will shelter you with his wings. His faithful promises are your armor and protection" (Psalm 91:4).

So why do I have cancer? Why is my child on drugs? Why did my husband leave me? Why did I lose my baby? Why can't I pay my bills?

If God promises to shelter and protect me, why isn't it happening? As Christians, why does it seem that we suffer the same illnesses, injuries and tragedies as the unbeliever?

Billy Graham said, "Nowhere does the Bible teach that Christians are exempt from the tribulations and natural disasters that come upon the world. Scripture does teach that the Christian can face tribulation, crisis, calamity, and personal suffering with a supernatural power that is not available to the person outside of Christ."

Just as the father runs alongside the wobbly bike as his son is learning to ride, God has positioned Himself very near to us, with His arms wide open, ready to catch us when we fall.

No one is free from suffering and adversity. There can be times when God seems very far away, and there doesn't seem to be hope that things will improve.

Sometimes God permits us to suffer so we can be an example to others, or possibly so we can share with others who are going through the same pain.

Christ didn't avoid the cross to escape the suffering. He knew that there was victory on the other side of the cross. If we lean on the Lord in our times of suffering, He will lead us to the victory on the other side. He will give us the strength we need to get through each day.

Through the Lord's mercies we are not consumed, because
His compassions fail not. They are new every morning;
Great is Your faithfulness. Lamentations 3:22

-Maureen McMahon

"For you have need of endurance, so that after you have done the will of God, You may receive the promise" (Hebrews 10:36).

Which is harder, to do or to endure? This question was asked by Amy Carmichael in one of the many letters she wrote to encourage others while in bed and in constant pain for the last twenty years of her life. She knew what it meant to endure.

For me it's definitely harder to endure. I am a doer! I like being busy and getting things done. For quite some time I have been going through a trial that makes the everyday things I once did with ease a lot more challenging. It feels as though life has been put on hold. Healing is slow in coming. It doesn't make sense to me to be in this place of waiting. It seems like time is being wasted. But as our wise pastor told me, nothing is wasted with God. He will redeem the time and use it for His glory. He's not done with me. He is preparing me. Yet I still struggle in the waiting. I wonder why it's such a long season.

Maybe in part it's about learning to endure, to be patient, and wait on the Lord's timing. Trusting His promises will be fulfilled even if they are delayed, and heaven is silent. Maturing in Him and growing in faith takes a lifetime, and at times involves struggle, strain, pain and a lot of tears. I have to trust even when it hurts and progress is slow.

I wonder sometimes if the Lord doesn't look at me, sigh, shake His head, and maybe even chuckle when I ask Him to please hurry and let this trial be over. He is not in a hurry, He wants me to wait and trust in His timing (which is perfect!) and rest in His love for me.

He's teaching me to endure.

-Denise Collinsworth

"...that you aspire to lead a quiet life, to mind your own business..." (1 Thessalonians 4:11-12).

It wasn't a typical Portland morning, but my attitude was like the drizzling weather common there-- incessant gray, dripping with silent complaints that the Lord heard loud and clear. That is when He answered me so loud in my spirit, I was startled, stunned even, by four crisp, clear, and kindly firm words, *"Mind your own business!"*

You see, my husband and I were about five years into our journey of infertility. Some procedures failed, and those that made great promises, we couldn't afford. I was desperate. I wanted to mortgage the house. But my husband refused (wisely, I might add) and I was angry with him.

Then my sister called. She was pregnant with her fourth child. Ouch. Managing a "Congratulations!" through quivering lips, I quickly hung up the phone and began to sob. It just wasn't fair. Didn't God care about me? Was something obstructing His view of me? I felt so forsaken and jealous, ready to plead my case before God, who somehow seemed to overlook me. Me! The stay-at-home wife with a house and a minivan for goodness sakes! Me! The faithful Christian girl and regular Bible study attendee.

Then He said it.

"Mind your own business."

"But..." I protested, so certain of my perfectly logical arguments.
"Mind your own business!" He replied, so certain of His perfect will.

I sighed in surrender, and finally listened.

"Don't I have the right to create the lives I want to, for My own purposes and glory, using whatever circumstances I choose?" He asked.

That immediately shut the mouth of my mind, the complaining in my spirit, and the self-pity and piety of my well-prepared protest.

"*Yes, Lord,*" I replied in my heart. In that moment of gentle brokenness, I could finally hear the truth of God's word, and with it came an illogical peace, and an unexplainable hope.

Forsaken? Not so.

"Let your conduct be without covetousness; be content with such things as you have. For He Himself has said, I will never leave you nor forsake you (Hebrews 13:5).

Forgotten? Not once.

"For I know the thoughts that I think toward you, says the LORD, thoughts of peace and not of evil, to give you a future and a hope." Jeremiah 29:11

Overlooked? Never.

"For the eyes of the LORD run to and fro throughout the whole earth, to show Himself strong on behalf of those whose heart is loyal to Him." 2 Chronicles 16:9

God sees me. He is gladly at work on His perfect plan in my life. He is minding MY own business. And truly, He works all things together for good for those who love Him.

Little did I know on that drizzly day in Portland, that five years later, the Lord would bring my sister and her four kids back to California. And within a few weeks, to our great surprise, we got a phone call informing us that my husband's company would be transferring him back to California as well. And these four kids about whom, I'm ashamed to admit, I complained to God about even creating, have become one of my greatest joys. Even while I railed against God's plan, all along He was minding my business-- He was creating lives that would one day fill my own empty arms.

Jesus has always been holding my life in the palm of His hand, whether I could see it or not. And it is in those palms that I see His dedication to me. This is where trust begins. Lean in, and look at the scars. Start here in minding your own business.

-Katie Bartrom

"For God has not given us the spirit of fear,
but of power and of love and of a sound mind"
(2 Timothy 2:7).

Cancer! "Carol, it doesn't look good" the doctor tells me over the phone. It's interesting the different emotions you go through when you hear this about your husband.

I did go weak at the knees, but was still trying to understand what she was telling me...*see an oncologist, PET Scan, CT Scan, biopsy.* My head is spinning, what did she say? I can't miss anything, I need to remember everything! I was overwhelmed, but knew I had to be strong for Bill and our girls and for about a day-and-a-half, I was.

Boy, that fear wants to attack and doesn't want to let go, but the thought kept coming to me 'the Bible says something about God not giving us the spirit of fear.' I couldn't wait to find it, and there it was just waiting for me in God's Word. Fear does not come from my Father. Even though I didn't think I could remember or keep track of all the new words and treatments and appointments, He has promised me a sound mind.

This verse was a lifeline, fear was never far, but never overwhelmed me. His promise of a sound mind was a great comfort as we navigated in uncharted waters. But it was His love that we felt every single day and came to realize that everything is under His Name, even the name of cancer.

-Carol Deckard

God is Enough!

"Do not turn aside from following the Lord . . . for then you would go after empty things which cannot profit or deliver, for they are nothing"
(I Samuel 12:20-21).

In the book of I Samuel, the Israelites cried out for an earthly king when they had a perfect heavenly Father who wanted to be their King. Even after He had proven His faithfulness by providing, protecting, and leading them, they still refused to believe He was enough. They wanted to be, and to look like, the other nations - to have an earthly king. God gave them their desire, but they soon realized their error.

There's something in our human nature that is not satisfied with God alone. We feel that we need something more; that He is not enough. Like the Israelites, we seek "things" that are *tangible* and *earthly*, that can take the place of God, but they leave us in a worse state because they are empty.

In John chapter 6, we read about a time when many disciples walked away from Jesus. When He asked the others who remained if they would leave also, Peter answered, "Lord, to whom shall we go? You have the words of eternal life. You are the Son of the Living God." Peter knew that there was no one else to run to. Only Jesus had eternal life to offer.

Finding our sufficiency in Christ alone is what is needed. Once we've established this in our hearts, we find that all else is empty and counterfeit. We must ask ourselves, "Do my actions and attitude demonstrate the belief that He is more than enough in every area of my life? Do I believe that I have everything I need in Him, and that I am complete in Him?

Let's not look to people, possessions, or "empty things", and expect to receive from them what only God can give. Let's look to Him and glorify His name by placing our trust in His love and sufficiency. Let's show the world around us - He is more than enough!

-Rebekah Caggegi

"Do Not Call Unclean What I Have Cleansed" (Acts 10:15).

Yesterday I spoke with two distraught young moms. They were swirling in guilt, fear and despondency. In both cases, lies and condemnation from the enemy was the culprit.

Condemnation is a vile trick of the enemy. The Bible says, "there is therefore NOW no condemnation to those who are in Christ Jesus" (Romans 8:1.) Nonetheless, satan slithers into our thinking with crippling accusations.

It was a privilege to point out to these precious sisters in Christ that their despondent thoughts of, "I'll never be a "good" Christian," were not coming from their Savior. God spoke to Peter, *do not call unclean what I have cleansed* (Acts 10:15). What followed was a miraculous outpouring of the Holy Spirit upon the Gentiles.

Dear reader in Christ, you are clean, redeemed, saved, set free, born again, and on a new course toward eternal life! We are chargeless in Christ. The Bible says, "Who shall lay ANY charge to God's elect?" (Romans 8:33).

We have no right to call something unclean that GOD has cleansed. He has cleaned you, washed you and redeemed you by the blood of His Son. You're clean! Refuse the lies of the enemy and feeble efforts to clean yourself up.

The Bible says, "If God kept a record of sins, who could stand?" (Psalm 130:3). God doesn't keep a record of your sins; satan does.

In Jeremiah 1:12, God says, "I am watching over MY Word to see that it is fulfilled." God watches over His promises to you, not your promises to Him. Jesus said, "NOW you are clean through the Word I have spoken to you." (John 15:3)

Do not call unclean what God has cleansed.

-Cindy Blackamore

"For you formed my inward parts;
You covered me in my mother's womb.
I will praise you, for I am fearfully and wonderfully made;
Marvelous are your works, and that my soul knows very well"
(Psalm 139:13-14).

After we were conceived, the gestation time for our arrival was approximately nine months. God knew the time and place we were to be born. His timing is perfect.

As I write this, the Lord is showing me how perfect his timing is. My husband was diagnosed with pancreatic cancer this year and began undergoing all the treatments needed. The doctors gave him six to nine months to live. Through the whole process, the Lord has shown me that as in birth, there is also a time for us to die.

Some of us will be taken quickly, but some of us will be given that time clock, with so many months or years before we go to be with Him.

I love it that our God is an orderly God, and He has a reason for everything. For any of you who have had a baby, I am sure you remember the labor pains before your precious baby was born. In death, there is a shutting down process before we go. And until our last breath, we have an opportunity to accept Jesus as our Savior. What a gift of grace He gives us.

For any of you who are going through a time when a physician may be giving you a timeline for your life, remember John 14:1-3: "Let not your heart be troubled; you believe in God, believe also in Me. In My Father's house are many mansions; if it were not so, I would have told you. I go to prepare a place for you. And if I go and prepare a place for you, I will come again and receive you to myself; that where I am, there you may be also."

-Cindy Martinez

"And we know that all things work together for good to them that love God, to them who are the called according to His purpose" (Rom. 8:28).

As I look back over my life, I see how God has used the sad and disappointing times, as well as the good times to build my faith and continue to mold me into the woman that He wants me to be. It's always easy to praise and thank God when the good things happen, but it's not until you have the unexpected heartbreaks and weather the storms of life, that you grow and learn to trust God in everything.

My mother was an amazing Christian woman, but the Lord allowed her to get cancer at the young age of 49. It was this heartbreaking diagnosis, that brought her three children back to the Lord.

It took the birth of four beautiful children to get a glimpse of the height and depth of God's love for his children. It took, and is still taking, that time and faith to see God's work (not mine) in their lives.

It took starting our own business and trying to make ends meet, to see that God would supply all of our needs. It takes the struggles that come with every passing day that let me put my faith, hope and trust in God. It is that faith and trust that continues to grow and lets me know that He sovereignly controls "my circumstances." I know that the growing pains are always very real.

Like it has been said before...without a little rain, how can a flower grow? In this I can trust....He said ALL things work together for good, not "all but one thing", or "some things work together", but "ALL things". Sometimes, I may grow weary, but His promises are always hidden in my heart, reminding me and encouraging me of His faithfulness and His work in my life, which in turn allows me to grow in my faith and trust in "everything" that He has set before me.

One of my mother's favorite poems says it all.

The Weaver

My Life, is but a weaving between my Lord and me.
I may not choose the colors; He knows what they should be;
For He can view the pattern upon the upper side,
While I can see it only; on this, the under side.

Sometimes He weaveth sorrow, which seemeth strange to me;
But I will trust His judgment, and work on faithfully;
Tis' He who fills the shuttle, He knows just what is best
So I shall weave in earnest and leave with Him the rest.

Not till the loom is silent and the shuttles cease to fly
Shall God unroll the canvas and explain the reason why--
The dark threads are as needful in the Weaver's skillful hand
as the threads of gold and silver in the pattern He has planned.
Author: Unknown

-Laurie Lusk

"I have told you these things so that in me you may have peace. In this world you will have trouble. But take heart, I have overcome the world" (John 16:33).

Do you ever feel like you are just waiting for the other shoe to drop? It seems like every week, we hear another friend has cancer, their marriage or children are in trouble and financial issues abound. This all confirms we are living in a fallen world.

In July of 1997, my husband and I were in my doctor's office receiving results from a recent biopsy I had just had due to a suspicious spot in my mammogram. We weren't expecting bad news, but when I heard him say, "You have breast cancer and need surgery" my head started spinning, I couldn't breathe, my heart was pounding. We asked if we could have a minute. As we stepped out of the office I prayed and asked the Lord, "what do I do I'm losing it here Lord". So much anxiety, I just couldn't get my head together. All of a sudden I heard God speak to me. "Choose Life, you're not dying today, I will be with you, DO NOT BE AFRAID!" A total peace came over me, and I knew He wouldn't leave me in this alone.

We went back into the office and told the doctor we were ready to set the date for my mastectomy. No anxiety, no fear. Only God can supply that kind of peace. I was in His hands, and there's no better place to be.

Jesus said, as long as we live in the world we're going to have trouble. We are not just in the world, we're in the world with Jesus, which makes it possible to overcome our trials and troubles. The day we accept Christ as our Savior, we become overcomers through Him! Knowing this, we can become more like Him. How? By knowing the God we serve, His character, His Word, who He is and why I can trust Him. Only then can we say, "Your will not mine." We can also be confident, that whatever we are going through, He will be going through it with us. (Deut 31:8) "And that all things work together for good for those who love God and are called according to His purpose" (Romans 8:28).

We will have many trials in our lives. Who we think Jesus is will determine how we go through those trials...our choice; will we be overcome or over-comers?

-Lynn deCamp

Psalm 139:1-12, Jeremiah 29:11

People park on the quiet street outside my bedroom window for many reasons: the phone call that needs to be answered, the argument that can't wait, or the police officer needing a break.

I've heard crying and cursing, tenderness and kindness. They have no idea that someone unintentionally hears their private conversations. Yet we have a God that not only intentionally hears our private conversations but also hears our every thought.

David wrote, "O Lord, You have searched me and You know me. You know when I sit and when I rise; You perceive my thoughts from afar. You discern my going out and my lying down; You are familiar with all my ways. Before a word is on my tongue, You know it completely, O Lord. Such knowledge is too wonderful for me, too lofty for me to attain. Where can I go from Your Spirit? Where can I flee from Your presence? If I go up to the heavens, You are there; if I make my bed in the depths, You are there. If I rise on the wings of the dawn, if I settle on the far side of the sea, even there Your hand will guide me, Your right hand will hold me fast. If I say, 'Surely the darkness will hide me and the light become night around me,' even the darkness will not be dark to You; the night will shine like the day, for darkness is as light to You!" What a comfort this is!

No matter what we are going through, the smooth and the difficult, the Lord knows and understands it all. He is deeply involved in the daily details of our lives and wants the best for us! His plans for us are good and not for evil, to give us a future and a hope!

-Elizabeth Downard

"He Comes After His Lost Sheep"
(Luke 15:4-7).

In a small back-woods Alabama town, she was taught godly principles in a Christian home, but she had wandered far from them. She thought she knew everything she needed to know about making a life for herself, but she quickly learned how wrong she was, and city living had taken its toll on her. She could not seem to get out of the miry clay of life and continued to sink deeper and deeper. Yet, in all of this, there was a line that she could not cross because of that early Christian foundation that was deep within her soul.

One day a woman, a total stranger, appeared in the doorway of her office and, without any introduction said, "The Lord told me to tell you, He wants His relationship back with you." Offended by the personal nature of such an encounter with a total stranger, she responded in an unfriendly tone, "You don't know me; you don't know anything about me!" With that, the stranger quickly departed. She ran after her, however, the stranger was nowhere to be found!!

As thoughts of the strange woman and her proclamation replayed over and over, days and weeks went by with no sign of the stranger. She began to think, "Could this have been an angel?" Then finally, in her office about a month later, she heard the stranger's voice again. She looked up and saw the woman standing in the doorway. The stranger said, "Can we go and talk?" Without hesitation, she responded, "Yes!"

As a result of that encounter, I rededicated my life to the Lord and have not turned back. I look forward to seeing my Savior's face, who came after me, His lost sheep; and to see my mother whose faithful prayers were answered. In the parable of Luke 15:4-7, Jesus says "what man of you, having a hundred sheep, if he loses one of them, does not leave the ninety-nine in the wilderness, and go after the one which is lost until he finds it?" If man is capable of such compassion for his lost sheep, how much more encouraged we can be in praying for our lost love ones. We can be assured that our Savior, with His tender and forgiving heart, will go after His sheep who is weary and wandering and receive that one unto Himself, as all of heaven rejoices!

-Carolyn Clark

"But without faith it is impossible to please Him, for he who comes
to God must believe that He is,
and that He is the rewarder of those who diligently seek Him"
(Hebrews 11:6).

This summer I had the privilege of taking fifteen 4th, 5th, and 6th graders to a week-long camp. There were a lot of activities such as swimming, archery, a zip-line, a giant swing, and much more. But our most precious time was our Bible study time. To see these young ones really grasp the understanding of our camp verse, Hebrews 11:6, was amazing. We also had to memorize the definition of faith. Faith believes God's word and acts upon it, no matter how we feel, because God promises a good result.

After I came home, that definition rang in my ears. Through every Bible study, I kept coming back to that definition, and in every circumstance, it was ringing in my ears. Let us have faith that pleases God. Stop listening to how you feel, because God's promises are true. He is the prize. Let our actions display the love of Jesus.

-Meg Schneider

Ephesians 5:31-32

It's a great mystery, but we the church are called the bride of Christ. One day we will meet Him face-to-face and will discover a new level of intimacy that is foreshadowed in a marriage relationship on earth.

Weddings always make me cry. Watching two hearts come together and wrap ribbons of love around each other in the presence of family and friends is such a joyous time. I love to watch the expressions on the bride's face as she walks toward her man and on the groom's as he gazes at her beauty. The kiss that seals their vows brings a spirit of rejoicing and hope for a happily ever after life of loving and serving each other.

But one of my very most favorite parts of the wedding celebration is the bride and groom dance. In each other's arms they sway to the music of their song and it is as if the world doesn't exist for those brief moments in time. It's just the two of them ~ the prince and princess at the ball.

Although some Christian denominations frown on dancing, the Bible tells of Old Testament men and women, including King David – a man after God's heart – dancing as a form of worship. Psalm 150:4 even commands us to praise Him with dancing.

One day as I reflected on what it would be like to dance with Jesus – that sweet intimate dance of the bride and groom – God spoke a truth into my spirit. *If you want to dance with Jesus, you have to let Him lead.*

Wow! Of course we know we're to follow Him as He guides and directs us in life. But suddenly that took on new meaning for me. A new perspective on what it feels like to really surrender.

Later that day, as I was stressing over something in my life and trying to solve it on my own, I felt Jesus tapping me on the shoulder.

"Did you want to sit this one out?" His spirit asked mine.

And suddenly I realized something. When I'm stressed and worried, I've stepped out of the dance, the one where He is leading and I am allowing His strong arms and hands to guide me.

"No, Lord. Hold me close and let's keep dancing." I closed my eyes and was back in His arms, swaying to the tempo of His heartbeat, and relaxing into His leading in my life.

Dear Lord,
My life is like a continuous dance, sometimes slow and graceful, other times fast-paced and noisy. Help me to remember that You are in the dance with me and want to lead me every step of the way.

-Rosemary Hines

"I know whom I have believed and am persuaded that He is able
to keep what I have committed to Him until that day"
(2 Timothy 1:12b).

We sing the song in church, "He makes beautiful things out of the dust, out of us." That's become my prayer over the past year-and-a-half since my dad passed away. The beginning of the song says, "All this pain, I wonder if I could ever find my way, I wonder if my life could really change at all. All this earth, could all that is lost ever be found, could a garden come up from this ground at all? " (by Gungor) The answer is, unequivocally, Yes!

What do you trust in when you find yourself in a painful place? May I suggest God's character and track record. Paul confidently stated that he was persuaded in whom he had believed. I too have been persuaded by The Lord and his faithfulness. He shows up in our grief. He plants his Word in our hearts, even when it looks as if nothing is happening. By His grace and love, He keeps His promises. With that, our faith soars and our hearts are built up in our most holy faith. While we hold on to His Word and wait in faith, we become a "testimony", standing and declaring to those around us what God has done on our behalf. We stand together in awe of God's goodness, loving care, protection, and faithfulness. Together as a body of women fulfilling our calling and destiny to glorify our Lord in the "Garden" of our lives.

The Lord knows what you are going through today. He faithfully takes us through the fire, valleys, heartaches, grief, chaos and pain as only He can. Amazingly, we come out the other side: stronger in faith, humbled that He hears and answers our prayers, confident in who He says He is, and filled with compassion for those going through the same heartache.

In the last year the Lord has taken my barren, weed infested yard and turned it into a beautiful garden. The roses are in full bloom, several are over seven feet tall. White, pink & red two-toned double delights and yellow and salmon colored roses line the driveway. Wildflowers have blossomed along the sidewalk along with orange poppies, fuchsia and pink daisies, black-eyed susans, purple bachelor buttons, and lavender zinnias. The most amazing are the mammoth sunflowers which are nearly nine feet tall with their bright, sunny faces looking to the sun.

Out of the dust the Lord has made something beautiful. It has solely taken seed, water, soil and the sun. God's Word is the seed. May I encourage you to plant His Word in your heart daily. Let His Spirit water it. Keep looking unto The Son. And He will cause your heart to spring forth into something beautiful.

-Miray Jaksa

"... 'The women of Zion are haughty, walking along with outstretched necks, flirting with their eyes, strutting along with swaying hips, with ornaments jingling on their ankles" (Isaiah 3:16).

Some things never change! We women always seem to fall into the trap of worrying far too much about how we appear and far too little about our character. Haughtiness is an especially deep and dark pit to fall into.

I remember plunging into the pool of pride back in the fourth grade. The "cool" girls at school started a *Pink Ladies* club (could have been my idea...folly is bound up in the heart of a child!) I still remember begging my mom for a pink jacket and asking her to sew the logo on the back. This was a serious club, and we wanted to stand out, to "walk along with outstretched necks" and consider ourselves better than others! The worst part of the club was not the jackets we wore, nor the activities we planned, but rather our haughty attitudes and pleasure at keeping other girls "out". We were like those women of Zion, walking, flirting, strutting, and jingling.

He who touched the lepers and rescued the woman caught in adultery and washed his disciples' feet has shown us a better way. The next time you get "dressed up", remember Peter's exhortation in 1 Peter 5:5b: "All of you, *clothe* yourselves with *humility* toward one another, because, 'God opposes the proud but gives grace to the humble.' "

-Nancy Tumbas

"O God, You have taught me from my youth; and to this day I
declare Your wondrous works.
Now also when I am old and gray headed, O God, do not forsake
me, until I declare Your strength to this generation,
Your power to everyone who is to come" (*Psalm 71:17*).

While reading a bedtime story to my four-year old grandson,
Ezekiel, he was leaning against me and rubbing my elbow. He
inquisitively asked "why is your elbow so bumpery"? After
pondering how to answer the little guy, I preceded to give him an
explanation. "Well my elbow has extra skin so I can bend it" I
demonstrated by moving it up and down. While I'm explaining,
he's rubbing first his elbow, then mine, giving them a thorough
investigation. He is forming his final conclusion to this situation,
and he replied shaking his little head "Noooo, your elbow is
bumpery because you're old and mine isn't because I'm new ." Yes,
it's true I have become a little bumpery. I am growing old I just can't
fight it.

God wants us to grow old wisely. Job said, "Is not wisdom found
among the aged? Does not long life bring understanding?" (Job
12:12). The lessons of hardship, success and failure we learn
in life should be passed on to the younger generation. "O God, thou
hast taught me from my youth: and hitherto have I declared thy
wondrous works" (Psalm 71:18). The silver lining to the cloud of
growing older is that regardless of the difficulties that come our
way we know from experience that if we lean on God and not our
own understanding, He will see us through..

What a blessing to be able to share all that God has taught us to our
GRANDCHILDREN.

-Lynna Ampe

"And if you give yourself to the hungry and satisfy the desire of the afflicted, then your light will rise in darkness and your gloom will become like midday. And the LORD will continually guide   you, and satisfy your desire in scorched places, and give strength to your bones; and you will be like a watered garden, and like a spring of water whose waters do not fail" (Isaiah 58:10-11).

Isaiah 58 begins with the Lord telling Isaiah to declare to the Israelites that they are living in sin. Although they are a righteous nation that delights in God, they cry out to him, asking Him why He does not notice their fast and humility. God tells them that their fast is about forcing their flesh to behave, but that the fast He chooses is completely different.

This is where it gets good!
Is this not the fast which I choose, to loosen the bonds of wickedness,
to undo the bands of the yoke, and to let the oppressed go free and break
every yoke?   Is it not to divide your bread with the hungry and
bring the homeless poor into the house; when you see the naked, to
cover him; and not to hide yourself from your own flesh?

God doesn't desire a fast where we focus on the flesh, and what we aren't supposed to do, He wants us to focus on the things that He HAS called us to do. Either way, we are denying our flesh, but only one way is positive and acceptable to the Lord; the other way is oppressive and counterproductive.

But, the scripture continues with promises and encouragement!

Then your light will break out like the down, and your recovery will
speedily spring forth; and your righteousness will go before you; the
glory of the LORD will be your rear guard. Then you will call and
He will say, 'Here I am'. If you remove the yoke from your midst, the
pointing of the finger and speaking wickedness,

Do you love that? The promise of Jesus is going before you as your righteousness and the glory of the Lord as your rear guard?

Could it get any better than that in a world of such uncertainty? Our call is simple, deny yourself; after that it could be hundreds of thousands of things every single day, but there is always a promise ... there is always that certain encouragement.

"And if you give yourself to the hungry and satisfy the desire of the afflicted, *then your light will rise in darkness and your gloom will become like midday. and the LORD will continually guide you, and satisfy your desire in scorched places, and give strength to your bones; and you will be like a well watered garden, and like a spring of water whose waters do not fail.*"

Isn't this what we all want? Why don't we accept it? Jesus paid the price; He bought us with His blood. Let's deny ourselves and live a life for Him, knowing that whatever the circumstances may look like, we will be a light in the darkness, and He will be our guide and our strength.

Let this be the beginning of a calling to deny ourselves, to deny the plans we have for ourselves and our future and to submit to His plan, not because we are forcing submission, but because we are answering the call He has placed on our lives – because we long to be a well-watered garden.

-Gretchen Hill

"Eye has not seen, nor ear heard, nor have entered into the heart of man, the things which God has prepared for those who love Him" (1 Corinthians 2:9).

This has always been one of my favorite verses because it is filled with hope of what is to come. We had this verse printed on our wedding invitations and it has held true after 18 years of marriage.

Even though I am very much in love with my husband, and love and adore our two sons God has given to us, I know that the best is yet to come. While we were singing the worship song, "Shout to the Lord," in church I wrote down one of the lines, "nothing compares to the promise I have in You." No matter how rough life gets down on earth we have the hope of our future in Christ. We know the end of the story, and it is more than what we can imagine. Our eyes have not seen what God has in store for us, both in this life and for eternity.

It is easy for me to keep my focus on the here and now and the trials and tribulations of this world, but as a Christian I need to look up and keep my focus on the end that is in store for "those who love Him." I love turning my attention to this verse and thinking about what life will be like living in heaven with my Savior. It makes all of the distractions of this world seem insignificant.

God is so good - I wanted to write this devotion so I could encourage my sisters in Christ, but God ended up blessing me. He gave me a "mountain-top experience" through this. Thank you, Lord!

I wanted to close with these lyrics from the worship song that touched me while doing this devotion:

"I sing for joy at the work of Your hands, forever I'll love you, forever I'll stand. Northing compares to the promise I have in You."

-Toni Gillespie

"Delight yourself in the Lord;
and He will give you the desires of your heart" (Ps. 37:4).

But Lord, if only I had a bigger paycheck, I could do so much more for You. If only I had a bigger house, we could let visiting missionaries stay with us. What about the cool pick up truck (I could help people move), or that beautiful horse – yes, that's the one! I want...I want...I can make it sound so holy.

Have you ever had this conversation with our precious Lord? I'm sure you've had similar conversations, maybe the truck and horse might not be on your wish list!

But really, when I read Psalm 37:4, I long to delight in my God He is after all, my heart maker. I've come to see this scripture differently of late. Instead of it being a formula on how to fulfill my "I wants", it's a marvelous way for Him to place new desires in my heart. The closer I am to Jesus, the more my heart's desires become His – He gives me (puts into my heart) His heart's desires.

So let's delight in our Lord! The results are glorious!

-Laura Hales

Where is your Focus?

A few years ago I entered "Little Red Hen" in our church cookbook. My mom, Bernice Hall, served it whenever we had company; it was her favorite dish. Along with the recipe, we were asked to provide our life scripture. After giving it some thought and prayer I decided on Philippians 4:6-7, "Be anxious for nothing...." At that time in my life, I was anxious about several situations. I knew rationally that it was wrong thinking. God has the very best in mind for us and we need to lay everything at His feet, but I was having a very difficult time doing that. Mom had fallen a few months after she turned 90 and was unable to live by herself anymore.

I had always heard that keeping a prayer journal was a good idea, so you can see how God is working in your life as He addresses each request. I began journaling and God indeed answered prayers for church friends, my husband, David, me and my mom, Bernie. I was beginning to really see how powerful prayer is.

My sister was working full days and staying with mom at night, with two other caregivers helping out. It was really taking its toll on my sister, physically, emotionally and financially (hiring and keeping caregivers, using mom's resources wisely, etc). I was here in California and went back to help mom as often as I could, but it was never enough for me. It was obvious that I could not control mom's condition or her future. I wanted so badly to see her recover - not decline and grow frail. This was the first time in my life that I not only felt totally helpless, but was unable to control the outcome of the situation. Thus began my journey of walking with the Lord like I never had before, asking and crying out to Him for guidance, in anguish and sorrow; and then, rejoicing with thanksgiving as He provided for mom and her needs.

For the last five years, every day I poured out my heart to God for my mom. Every day I would pray with Mom, asking God for His blessings to be upon her, standing on His promise that He will never leave her or forsake her. As the years went by, my prayers were answered for proper care, for provision, and for what used to be taken for granted (that she could breathe easily and speak clearly, etc). The ultimate and final prayer was answered early in the morning, August 7, 2013 when her Lord and Savior Jesus Christ, wrapped His arms around my precious mom, Bernie, and took her home to be with Him. She died like she lived, calmly, peacefully, with quiet strength and dignity. She was teaching me up until her last breath.

Just the other day God spoke to me about my life. The verse 2 Corinthians 5:7 came to me "For we walk by faith, not by sight." As my mom declined, I saw my only hope was my faith in God and His promises. I had finally taken my eyes off of myself and put them where they needed to be - on Jesus Christ.

-Terri Elia

Proverbs 31: 10-31

I remember studying this chapter of the Bible as a young newlywed. I was so intimidated by the Godly wife that was described…. she was so perfect! Some days I felt as though I gave generously to the poor but what about the day I wasn't an early riser? Did that mean I didn't qualify as a Proverbs 31 woman for my husband? It caused me a lot of anxiety…

If I can be so bold as to briefly summarize her accomplishments:

1. She gives her husband confidence
2. She brings good, not harm
3. She works with her hands
4. She provides delightful food
5. She is an early riser so as to provide for all her household
6. She is a shrewd investor
7. She is a hard worker
8. She tends to her home and pocketbook so that there are no shortages in either
9. She is generous to the poor and needy
10. She provides for her family's clothing needs
11. Her husband is respected because of her
12. She is clothed with strength and dignity
13. She doesn't fear emergencies because she is prepared
14. She speaks wisdom
15. She is not idle

Of course, this woman is a wife and a mother, but the appeal and the encouragement are to any woman. This is the standard to which we as Christian women are to aspire. Having said that, I have often reminded young new brides who fret about some perceived deficiency in themselves that their husbands married them because they are beloved of their husbands. A man doesn't marry a woman because she has a job and can provide for him or because she is a great cook; a man marries a woman because she is HIS Proverbs 31 lady. Verse 11 brings us the first clue in what makes you your husband's Proverbs 31 woman... "the heart of her husband trusts in her." Another version states, "Her husband has full confidence in her." We can all do that as wives! I think this is so overlooked in marriages and society in general today. A husband is usually portrayed in movies and the media as a bungler who needs a woman to come along and fix all the chaos he has created. No wonder a Proverbs 31 woman is to be praised! What husband would fail to adore a wife who gives him confidence and in whom his heart trusts?

The other attributes are also very important, and I should note here that this wife is never idle. We are told this repeatedly and it is the last attribute listed before the blessings of her family. Lest we miss the point, we are also told she "sets about her work vigorously." She is the important, multi-tasker who makes her house a home.

But the main point to me of this chapter is summed up nicely in verse 30, "Charm is deceptive, and beauty is fleeting; but a woman who fears the Lord is to be praised."

So all of my worry about not measuring up to this standard earlier in my life is silly! We women who love the Lord are to strive to please Him, and by studying His Word, we are transformed by the fruit of the Spirit into our own unique version of God's Proverbs 31 woman.

What a blessing!

-Catherine Griffin

"My strength is made perfect in weakness"
(2 Corinthians 12:9).

Since my earthly father has never been a nurturing, affectionate, there-for-me kind of dad, I grew up to be self-sufficient, not asking or expecting anything from anyone. Because of this, it has never been easy for me to relate to my Heavenly Father as my Abba Father.

This summer my dad visited us for two months. It's been a long time since I've been with him for that length of time. It was extremely hard on me because I learned more things about him that I disliked and it brought the worst out in me. I found myself struggling with anger, bitterness, hurt feelings, and desiring to hurt him with my words. Praise God for my faithful friends who were praying for me.

One friend told me to pray for compassion. I didn't like the feeling of weakness in my hurt, little girl's heart so it was easier to be angry, but I knew I wasn't pleasing the Lord. I started asking Him to give me compassion towards my dad. As I prayed day after day, I realized I wasn't so angry anymore; hurt, yes, but through it all I've learned that my Heavenly Father loves me when I'm unlovable; He is always there and has always been there for me. I can rest in that, continue to pray for my earthly father, and see that in the times that I'm weak that is when the Lord gives me His perfect strength.

Is there a time in your life that God has had to break you of your strength so that His strength is visible?

-Becky Araoz

"But as the days of Noah [were], so also will the coming of the Son of Man be. For as in the days before the flood, they were eating and drinking, marrying and giving in marriage, until the day that Noah entered the ark, and did not know until the flood came and took them all away, so also will the coming of the Son of Man be. Then two [men] will be in the field: one will be taken and the other left. Two [women will be] grinding at the mill: one will be taken and the other left. Watch therefore, for you do not know what hour your Lord is coming. But know this, that if the master of the house had known what hour the thief would come, he would have watched and not allowed his house to be broken into. Therefore you also be ready, for the Son of Man is coming at an hour you do not expect" (Matthew 24:37-44 NKJV).

My sister, Sherry, was diagnosed with cancer in May 2013. My sisters and I threw a party for Sherry's 71st birthday on May 27. It was a blessed event since the sisters hadn't seen each other in a while. We knew the next time all four of us would be together would be in heaven. Sherry went to heaven on June 30, 2013.

The day of her memorial service, July 6, I heard from my dad's neighbor that he wasn't doing well. He died on July 12, 2013. My heart sank when I heard the news. I had prayed so many times for his salvation and tried to explain God's gift of salvation to him. I can only hope in his last few hours that he believed.

What a difference it is to know that a person is ready to meet God when they die. I know I'll see my sister again but I can only hope I will see my dad again. I know God's grace far surpasses my pea-size brain and I know there will no longer be tears in heaven; but, oh, how I wish I had that same assurance about both of my loved ones. In Matthew 24, God reminds us that in the days of Noah before the flood people were living their lives and unaware a flood was to come and take them all away. There's a warning here also – people will be working and some will be taken and others left behind. God tells us to be ready when Jesus returns. We never know when our appointed time to pass from this earth is. We need to be ready to meet Jesus....either in heaven or when He returns to this earth. Do you believe in Jesus? Are you ready to meet Jesus?

-Anita Lucarelli

Christ-Like Communication

"May the words of my mouth and the meditation of my heart be pleasing to You, O Lord my Rock and my Redeemer" (Psalm 19:4).

Some women love to talk! I can respect this because I'm one such woman. I speak many words throughout the day, but what am I really saying? Am I speaking words that encourage those around me? Am I speaking words of healing that build up those that God has blessed my life with? Am I displaying the fruit of His Spirit living in me? I struggle with this myself, so my heart goes out to women who struggle with expressing themselves in a correct manner.

Research has shown that an average woman can speak 7,000 words a day, use an additional 2,500 vocal sounds to communicate (such as grunts and huffs), and use about 9,000 non-verbal responses (such as facial expressions, head movements, and other body language signals).

We are saying a lot in our day! We need to express ourselves in ways that honor the Lord. Determine to be a woman who communicates only in ways that will please the heart of Jesus.

My prayer is this:

Lord, my desire is to please you in all ways. Help me to be aware of what comes out of my mouth and lies deep in my heart. In Your Name, Amen.

-Christi Terry

"…and if children, then heirs-heirs of God and joint heirs with Christ, if indeed we suffer with Him, that we may also be glorified together" (Romans 8:17).

You may know this truth intellectually, that God is your Father, but may not have allowed yourself time to soak in it emotionally. Our Father is the King of Kings! We have been adopted! The Bible says that we're joint heirs with Christ, and He is the Prince of Peace. That makes us, beloved, into born-again princesses.

Next time you are at church, look around. See the crowns sparkling under the fluorescent lights. I like to 'see' every sister with one on their beautiful heads as I speak with them, no matter how old, no matter how new their walk with Him…yes, even the lady who drives me nuts. They are royalty - princesses of the King…anointed and gifted in Him. To speak ill of another would be…well, it would be treasonous. Try to 'see' the figurative crown that will ultimately be placed there by our precious one-and-only Living Hope. Look closer…it's there.

When you pray, day by day, ask God to show you how He sees others…ask Him to allow you to see without comparison, but with compassion.

-Audra Moraga

"For I know the plans that I have for you declares the Lord, plans
for welfare and not for calamity to give you a
future and a hope" (Jeremiah 29:11).

You are exactly where God wants you to be today! He has a plan
and a purpose for your life! Sometimes, the road is smooth and
everything seems right and wonderful; at other times, the road is
difficult and rocky and it seems like our world is falling apart at the
seams.

God loves us with an unfailing love. His mercies are new every
morning. He cares about all the details of our lives, the struggles,
the pain, and the sorrow! He promises to take all of the situations in
our lives, the good, the bad, the hurtful, and to use them for good.
He does not promise us a life of comfort, or a life without pain. He
promises that He will never leave or forsake us (Hebrews 13:5). He
promises that all things will work together for our good (Romans
8:28).

We can trust our God with our lives. We can trust that He will lead
us and guide us. Our God loves us so much that He sent His son to
die for us. Jesus suffered the shame and pain on the cross and took
our place, so that our sins would be forgiven and we might have
eternal life. We have a God who loves us! We have a God who has
promised that He would provide for all of our needs (Philippians
4:19). We have the hope of heaven!

-Penny Newman

Trust in the LORD with all your heart,
And lean not on your own understanding;
In all your ways acknowledge Him,
And He shall direct! your paths (Proverbs 3:5-6).

Growing up in a family of ten children with a single mom brought so much fear and uncertainty in my life. As I got older, I grew closer to the Lord and hid His Word in my heart. His Word became my comfort and strength.

There have been so many other situations in my life where God will remind me of this verse, and it is true:

*<u>Trust</u> the Lord
*Don't lean on what <u>you</u> think
*Acknowledge <u>Him</u>
*He will work it <u>all</u> out

This verse has taught me that God doesn't make mistakes, regardless of your circumstances. If we truly love Him, we <u>will</u> trust Him.

-Lupe Lee

"You are the salt of the earth; but if the salt loses its flavor,
how shall it be seasoned?
It is then good for nothing but to be thrown out and trampled
underfoot by men"
(Matthew 5:13).

I came across this familiar passage spoken by Jesus and it stood out to me as a reminder and an exhortation of the responsibility that is mine to remain strong in my faith and to be an example to those who do not know Him. Jesus calls us the "salt of the earth". Salt, as defined in Webster's Dictionary has many uses. It is used for seasoning and preserving. It gives tang or piquancy to anything. Most importantly, it is something that   preserves,   purifies or corrects.

In this world, the tenets of the Bible are perceived as harsh, uncompromising, and outdated. Sin is no longer seen for what it is and if we allow ourselves to be lured into believing what the world believes or if we refuse to stand up and defend what we know is right and true, we are guilty of rejecting our Savior and His Words in Matthew 5:16, "Let your light so shine before men, that they may see your good works and glorify your Father in heaven."

We are the only Bible that many people see, and how we live our life is our testimony to those around us. May God help us to be strong and bold as we serve Him.

-Jan Browning

In case of emergency you may choose to dial 911, or even better, you may thumb to Psalm 91:1.

You may be having a bad day. You may have received disturbing news, or perhaps you are simply feeling fearful and not up to the task at hand. You may be physically or mentally exhausted or you may just be feeling that you can't go on any longer.

Knowing that at any time you can call up for help and get immediate Heavenly attention may relieve you of all the terrors of the night. Do get under the shadow of the Almighty God. He will deliver you. He will cover you with His feathers where you can take refuge under His wings. No evil shall befall you; no evil should come near your dwelling.

What a better course of action than calling upon your Almighty Father and only God! Try Him. He is available 24/7 to come to your rescue.

Psalm 91:1 "He who dwells in the secret place of the most High shall abide under the shadow of the Almighty."

-Francine Girard

"Trust in the LORD with all your heart, and do not lean on your own understanding" (Proverbs 3:5).

One of the chores I dread most is changing the fitted sheet on our bed. It sounds silly but I always manage to expend more energy than I should wrestling to get it on. One morning, as I was taking on this daunting task and struggling to get the last corner of the sheet onto the mattress, I heard a voice in my head, "you're doing it wrong". I have come to recognize that gentle, soft voice. "Lord, I think I've got this, I've done it plenty of times". Flustered, I stepped back and saw I was doing it wrong. "Okay Lord, I hear you". I pulled the sheet off, turned it around, and started over - it fit perfectly.

I was particularly convicted in that moment because my husband and I are facing a big decision for our family. I have to admit that I have wrestled with more than just bed sheets for the last few months. I've wrestled with anxiety and fear over this big decision. I was reminded of that hymn *His eye is on the sparrow.* In that moment, God was calling out to me and reminding me that even in the simplest of tasks, He has me covered. He cares for me. I may not fully understand the circumstances in the trials or big decisions that we face, but God does. Right now it is a season of uncertainty but I rejoice because I trust God's certainty, that *all things work together for good for those who love Him and have been called by His purpose* (Romans 8:28).

This is an awesome season, a time when we are trusting God with all of our heart, knowing that He is bigger than any decision or trial…even wrestling a fitted sheet.

-Marty Davis

"Through the Lord's mercies we are not consumed,
Because His compassions fail not.
They are new every morning;
Great is Your faithfulness (Lam 3:22-23).

Oh, what a beautiful morning!

There is nothing like the cool morning air, as you rise early to meet the day. Opening the back doors, the quietness and stillness is so evident that you can actually hear yourself think.

The world is seemingly calm and you have a sense that all is well. Bits of sunlight filter through the coastal clouds. Birds begin to sing as though they are praising our Creator for their wonderful lives. Flowers start to open up as the dew begins to dry on their petals.

Jesus is on your mind and all that He has done for you comes to memory. You are touched as you open up His Word, to bring meaning to your day. You walk away with confidence in who you are in Him.

Wait there is a turn of events. What about that morning that is woken with an unexpected phone call, or a situation that throws you for a curve? There is an argument that erupts out of nowhere. There is a battle raging, a war ensuing and a struggle within. Sometimes it's just the old nature creeping back in.

There is still time dear saint. His mercies are new every morning. Stop, turn around and look at your choices. Ask yourself, whom will I serve this day? Recognize that the Lord is with you in the still waters and the raging seas. The victory is yours to have when you keep your gaze on Jesus.

Let His Spirit reign in you, moment by moment, by your devotion and surrender and He will bring peace once again to your morning. Psalm 5:3

-Micki Rocha

"Why are you cast down, O my soul? And why are you disquieted within me?
Hope in God, for I shall yet praise Him
for the help of His countenance" (Psalm 42:5).

Lord you know me very well, much better than I know myself. You also know the valley that I am in and all the struggles and challenges I am facing. Sometimes I wish I had stayed on the mountaintop and had never come down into this valley. But at the same time, I know that You always have my best interests in mind, which might not always be the experiences I want to have, or the places that I want to be.

I know that sometime soon, or not so soon, this season of my life will end and another season will start. It is up to me to either choose to learn all that You have for me during this time, or just whine and have self-pity. Lord, I need You much more than ever before, I need to lean on You, and I need to talk with You constantly. I need to meditate on Your love, your sacrificial selfless love, and your promise. I praise you for all that you have done for me and all that You are doing for me.

Though sometimes my eyes cannot see well, my ears cannot hear well, and my feet cannot walk properly because of weakness, pain and sleepless nights, I know that joy comes in the morning!

"Oh, send Your light and Your truth! Let them lead me;
Let them bring me to Your holy hill and to Your tabernacle."
Psalm 43:3

"For I shall yet praise Him the help of my countenance
and my God." Psalm 43:5b

-Linda Varda

"Seek the LORD and his strength; seek His presence continually! Remember the wondrous works that He has done, His miracles, and the judgments He uttered"
(Psalm 105:4-5/ 1 Chronicles 16:11-12).

The commands here are straightforward enough, right?

Straightforward, yes, but stunning also.

Our Lord calls us to seek Him and test His faithfulness by remembering all He has said and done. In this, He says, "everything about Me proves that you can seek Me and find all that you need. Just try Me."

We are more than artwork God glances at occasionally. We are His family and His body. Not only does He allow us to seek Him, but He asks us to do so while offering us continual strength and communion.

As stunning as that is, so often I ask God to increase MY strength not thinking to ask for HIS strength. How silly! Why do we ask for more of our own strength when He offers us His? When we ask for Him to build up human strength, where is our focus? Certainly not on what He can do. We're bound by what we cannot do.

God asks us to surrender our struggles and take hold of His mighty hand, remembering and rejoicing in the truth that He is able to do all things. And what a privilege it is to do so!

-Elizabeth Marsh

"And if one member suffers, all the members
suffer with it..."
(I Corinthians 12:26).

One Sunday, I picked up some materials from Open Doors Ministry off the information table at church. Included was a rubber barbed wire bracelet to remind me to pray for persecuted Christians. I put it on and prayed throughout the day. The next morning when I woke up and saw the black barbed wire that encircled my wrist, my stomach turned, a feeling I couldn't shake for the entire day; the pain and torment symbolized by the barbed wire sank in and resonated in my I heart. I didn't want to wear it anymore, but I kept it on to remind myself to pray for my hurting sisters and brothers in Christ. My mind went to the verse, "if one member suffers, all the members suffer with it." I knew this verse in my head but it wasn't until the day I put on the bracelet that it penetrated my heart.

I have not known the kind of suffering those who are being persecuted experience, but the constant reminder around my wrist brought me, ever so slightly, into the fellowship of suffering with them. Wearing the bracelet continually reminds me to pray and brings me closer to those who are hurting.

-Sabrina Klinck

Will you believe?

"Now faith is being sure of what we hope for and certain of what we do not see" (Hebrews 11:1).

It's easy to believe in what is understandable, proven, and seen, but what about all the things we don't have answers for? What about our problems, our hurts, and the hurts of this world? Can we ever understand fully what God is doing?

Think for a moment. What if all the unanswerable questions in your mind were answered? Would you still believe? What if all your problems and the problems of this world were answered? Would you still believe? For some, the answer would still be no. You can know everything about God and still not believe. Why? It takes faith.

Do you have faith to believe in a God you will never fully understand? Do you have faith to believe in God when things don't go your way and life throws you into the pits? Do you have faith to believe in a God who won't give you answers to all your questions?

It's easy to fall into a cynical mindset and question the validity of who God is, of what God is, and why God allows things to happen the way they do. Forget all that and imagine a perfect world. Would you still believe?

When the going gets tough or when life is great, will you still believe? Do you have the faith it takes to believe? Will you ask God to give you this faith, which only He can give?

-Sylvia Yeung

"Because you have kept My command to persevere, I also will keep you from the hour of trial which shall come upon the whole world, to test those who dwell on the earth. Behold, I am coming quickly! Hold fast what you have, that no one may take your crown" (Revelation 3:10-11).

Because I do my best to be faithful and try to cling to God, He will keep me whether it is through trials or from trials. If I hold fast and cleave to Him, I will abide with Him wearing a victor's crown. I'll get to see Him face to face someday; He gives me strength for the here and now... "come what may." God has seen me through so much in my life, giving me strength and joy. I am foolish to ever doubt Him.

-Tamara Munsell

In the multitude of my anxieties within me,
Your comforts delight my soul" (Psalm 94:19).

This verse is a necessary, gentle daily reminder to me, especially with my busy schedule and everything that is happening in my life while I'm going through my first year of college. I know that it is God whom I need to put my trust in. Even with all my anxiety and the daily worries, He will delight my soul in the most troublesome times, no matter how big or small.

-Paige Schneider

Sunflower and Coconut
"Because you are my help, I sing in the shadow of your wings"
(Psalm 63:7).

My whole family was so excited! It had been a year-and-a-half since we first raised baby chicks into adult hens, but now we were introducing two new chicks, whom we named Sunflower and Coconut, to our small flock. Daisy, our beautiful golden-laced Wyandotte, was broody - AGAIN - and this time we needed to do something to help her. Like broody hens everywhere, she was losing weight, not eating or drinking enough, and sitting in a nesting box day and night, ruffling out her feathers and screeching when bothered, all because she wanted to hatch some chicks. So, because we don't have a rooster, we resorted to buying some tiny chicks to trick her into thinking she had hatched them. Those two little peeping puffs of fluff were so cute! My family felt guilty risking their little lives as we slipped them under a sleeping Daisy's tummy that night. I'm sure I wasn't the only one in my family praying for their safety all night! Would they run out from under Daisy and die of the cold? Have a run-in with a critter who wanders into the coop? Get pecked by the adult chickens, or even rejected by Daisy, herself?

We anxiously raced outside the next morning to find a happy new mother hen plus two cheeping babies hopping around her. It had worked! And what fun we had watching Daisy teach Sunflower and Coconut how to eat, drink, peck around the yard, and take time to rest. She would sound out a quick succession of short little "bock bock bocks" to call her little ones back under her or to get their attention for their next lesson. My family didn't get as much work done around the house those days as we watched them and marveled at how God created such amazing animals.

Not only did Sunflower and Coconut huddle under Daisy's feathered-out body for warmth, but one day, we witnessed Coconut pop her white head out from under Daisy's wing. What a precious sight! I couldn't help but recall Psalm 63:7, a Bible verse I have always loved, especially because I am a control-freak.

I tend to get bossy around my house, take charge, and plan, plan, plan. I'm just not the kind of person who feels that I can relax and allow someone else to lead in the everyday matters of living (I am married to a natural follower who makes the final decisions in the family as the husband, but is happy to yield to my overall direction on daily things at home). While I like to be in control of my home and our schedule, it does get tiring at times. Even when we finally go on a vacation, I still feel like I'm at work, planning, guiding, explaining the itinerary, guiding us from one place to the next, etc.

But what a comfort to know that no one holds it all together better than the Lord! I am able to rest in the security that at any time I can crawl under his loving "wings," and even sing under His able protection, no matter what storm may be brewing around me. He has all my steps ordered and knows my own needs better than I do. I am so glad that He, the Lord of the universe, my precious Jesus, will keep me warm, safe, feeling secure, and personally loved.

Unfortunately, despite Daisy's attentive care, both Sunflower and Coconut died of a problem that often plagues baby chicks. We all miss their presence, and I am grateful that they helped break Daisy's broodiness. Yet, I am most thankful for the visual image that the Lord provided through them: a sweet, memorable picture of His warm, caring protection over us while we are free to sing - or "cheep" - in the shadow of His wings.

-Kim Hensley

A Princess Forevermore

When I was a little girl, I dreamed of being a princess. My prince charming would come in and rescue me, and we would live happily ever after. However, after many years of living in the reality of a "sin-filled" life, I lost my little girl hopes and dreams. It wasn't until I came to faith in Christ Jesus in my early twenties that I realized that God had heard and answered the desires of my little girl heart. My Father is The King. My Christ is my Prince Charming who rescued me from the punishment of my sins, and I am forevermore a princess in a kingdom that will never end. Now, that's a happy ending! Today, I hope you embrace your inner princess as I have and realize the love that we have in God the Father and His Son, Jesus Christ.

Precious in His sight – (Isaiah 43:4)

Riches and honor – (I Chronicles 29:12)

In His love – (John 15:10)

No other way into the Kingdom of God – (John 14:6)

Calm Spirit – (Proverbs 17:27)

Enter into His courts with thanksgiving – (Psalm 100:4)

Shows fruit – (Galatians 5:22)

Sings a song of salvation – (Exodus 15:2)

-Christi Terry

"Now as they were traveling along, Jesus entered a certain village and a woman named Martha welcomed Him into her home And she had a sister called Mary, who moreover was listening to the Lord's word, seated at His feet. But Martha was distracted with all her preparations and she came up to Him, and said, "Lord, do you not care that my sister has left me to do all the serving alone? Then tell her to help me..' But the Lord answered and said to her, "Martha, Martha, you are worried and bothered about so many things, but only a few things are necessary, really only one, for Mary has chosen the good part, which shall not be taken away from her"
(Luke 10:38-42).

I love this -- "You are worried and bothered about so many things!" How many times have we allowed ourselves to worry and fret over seemingly small issues in our lives?   In the end the Lord works it all out, according to His purposes, and we find that there was no need to worry in the first place.

Let's choose to be a Mary today -- Let's choose not to worry and be bothered!   Let's choose to spend time with Jesus and sit at His feet! <u>This is where we find peace</u>!!

-Penny Newman

SEEKING GOD
C.O.N.S.T.A.N.T.L.Y.

It's Sunday morning, and a little girl stands at the curb in front of her house while her mother watches from the kitchen window. She's wearing a pretty handmade dress and white gloves. In her hands are the small white Bible given to her by her grandmother and a few coins for the offering. "Oh, please let someone stop and offer me a ride to church," she thinks to herself. Not fully understanding the stirring in her heart, she waits expectantly and hopes. Most Sundays a willing neighbor stops to give her a ride. She never knows which church will be her final destination. Some weeks it's the Presbyterian or Lutheran, while other weeks it might be the First Christian or Southern Baptist.
SEEKING.

This little girl is about 10 years old when the Billy Graham Crusade comes to town. Her parents don't take her to church, so she's certain they won't take her to the Crusade. She asks around the neighborhood in search yet again for a willing neighbor to give her a ride. Once inside the stadium, she climbs to the very top in order to have a perfect view. There she sits all alone, taking in every word. Exiting the stadium, she spots a table set up with brochures and pictures of the Graham family. She eagerly signs her name to the list in hopes an autographed 8X10 picture will be sent her way. Weeks later it arrives. She quickly places the treasured keepsake under her mattress where she can longingly touch and peek at it when she kneels by her bedside to pray.
SEEKING GOD.

Years pass. Seeds planted lay dormant. The little girl seeking God grows up and becomes a woman seeking God. Yet again, someone takes her to church where she meets Jesus and invites Him into her heart. She wonders if anyone ever personally told her about Jesus but quickly realizes missed opportunities in the past aren't important compared to decisions made today. Though she can't remember the words of Billy Graham that day years ago at the Crusade, she's certain they created a thirst and a desire in her heart. She's thankful for every ride to church and appreciates the faithfulness of God to protect and guide her. She yearns to serve Him all the remaining days of her life.
SEEKING GOD CONSTANTLY.

> *Lord, thank you for caring for me when I was*
> *lost and seeking. Now I seek to know your*
> *plans for my life. May I never miss an*
> *opportunity to share your love with*
> *others ... especially children with*
> *hungry hearts standing on a curb.*

May I remain a woman SEEKING GOD CONSTANTLY.

-Candy Ohanian

"But we all, with unveiled face, beholding in a mirror the glory of the Lord, are being transformed into the same image from glory to glory, just as from the Lord, the Spirit."
(2 Corinthians 3:18).

"Transformation." It was such a clear word from a familiar voice. "I'm changing you from the inside out." My family recently had a huge change in our lives. Suddenly my dad was diagnosed with pancreatic cancer. Within a month and a day the Lord took him home to glory. A whirlwind of activity soon followed. We had to plan a memorial service, do a quick remodel on the 1960 home of my parents, and prepare our townhouse for the rental market. Slowly we have been updating and decorating my childhood home. It's been an emotional journey through the valley of the shadow of death, but the Lord has been ever present and faithful. With all the change that has taken place, there have been blessings along the way: God's comfort through family at church, helping hands of friends to paint and organize, and the prayers of the saints which have kept and sustained us in the grief.

Besides the interior of our home, a total transformation is taking place in the front yard, (which is a very good thing). The kelly green trim my dad had painted on the house is now an inconspicuous off-white. The weeds that had taken over the lawn are gradually diminishing. Even the two oversized front doors received a make-over from kelly green to stately black. Flowers have been planted to add color and beauty. Each day it is a work in progress.

Overall, the transformation has been good, but it reminds me of the greater transformation taking place within my own heart. More than ever The Lord has shown me that this world is not my home. My dad lived in this house for forty-five years and nearly thirty of those years were with my mom. It goes without saying that He didn't take anything with Him. All his stuff is still here.

The Lord is in the process of changing us from the inside out, just like my home presently. He works in our hearts lovingly, and gently, with a holy goal in mind. Jesus is the best interior designer of all time. If you are going through your own transformation process, trust Him in faith. Give Him total control to change you from the inside out. Allow Him to comfort you through His Word and by those near to you. Cry out to him in your pain, and He will hear you as you draw near to Him. He's doing a Holy Transformation in you- from glory to greater glory. One day soon, in the not too distant future, we'll see Him face to face. And the things we suffer here will all be worth it when we cross the finish line of heaven, like my dad.

"Therefore we do not lose heart, but though our outer man is decaying, yet our inner man is being renewed day by day. For momentary, light affliction is producing for us an eternal weight of glory far beyond all comparison, while we look not at the things which are seen, but at the things which are not seen; for the things which are seen are temporal, but the things which are not seen are eternal" (2 Corinthians 4:16-18).

-Miray Jaksa

"He has made everything beautiful in His time
also He has put eternity in their hearts" (Ecclesiastes 3:11 (a).

I was thinking about this scripture last week and my thoughts turned to my daughter's journey to parenthood. By the age of 16 my daughter was told she wouldn't be able to have children. Heartbreaking, yes, but all along she knew God had a plan for her and that she had to keep her eyes on the promise that He knows the plans He has for her and they were for good and not evil, to give her a future and a hope (Jer. 29:11).

My daughter met the love of her life at 21, and they were married at 22. Her husband knew she would not be able to have children and although they would love to have a family, they decided whatever God had for them is what they wanted and they would wait to see what doors He would open.

My daughter became a teacher at the school she attended as a child and always said, "Look at all the children God has given me!" She was content in her circumstances. Right before her 30th birthday, she found out she was expecting a child, but already there were problems. My daughter was confined to bed rest until the crisis passed. My daughter and her husband welcomed a beautiful baby girl in May of the next year. They were blessed.

Of course it wasn't long before they wanted to add to their family. It seemed it wasn't meant to be. In the course of the next six years, five babies were lost and most were in the second trimester. In her sixth pregnancy, at the beginning of her third trimester, they went for her check-up and she was told there wasn't a heartbeat. They scheduled her to go to the hospital where they would induce labor to deliver this baby.

The challenge was heartbreaking at the time but the blessing would be in heaven for eternity. (Eccl 3:11a) They chose to believe and trust that God knew what was best for them.

There is also a very happy ending to my daughter's story. They welcomed another little girl the following year. She was unexpected, but a beautiful finish to the family God gave them. She came in God's perfect timing.

-Lynn deCamp

"But his delight is in the law of the Lord and on His law he meditates day and night" (Psalm 1:2).
"Thy Word is a lamp unto my feet and a light unto my path" (Psalm 119:105).

My friends, Claudia and Allen, love to camp in exotic places. They also enjoy reading numerous books on how to stay safe while camping. On their honeymoon, they decided to camp in the Serengeti. They drove their Jeep about 100 miles into the park before stopping for the night and setting up their tent. In the morning, they got up and unzipped the tent. Not ten feet away was a pride of lions sitting under a tree watching them! They talked about what they should do and decided they should make a run for it to the Jeep. They knew it would be the safest thing to do, but they would have to leave their tent and supplies behind.

Thankfully, they made it to the Jeep safely! Just like Claudia and Allen meditated on their camping books, we need to be meditating on the Word of God. We need to be "students" of the Bible. Scripture gives us clear guidance and direction, and it gives us wisdom in every area of our life. We can be prepared for anything that comes our way. So when you have to run from that spiritual pride of lions, be confident that His Word will be *a lamp unto your feet and a light unto your path.*

-Elizabeth Downard

"The hand of the LORD was on me, and he brought me out by the Spirit of the LORD and set me in the middle of a valley; it was full of bones. He led me back and forth among them, and I saw a great many bones on the floor of the valley, bones that were very dry. He asked me, "Son of man, can these bones live?" I said, "Sovereign LORD, you alone know." Then he said to me, "Prophesy to these bones and say to them, 'Dry bones, hear the word of the LORD! This is what the Sovereign LORD says to these bones: I will make breath enter you, and you will come to life. I will attach tendons to you and make flesh come upon you and cover you with skin; I will put breath in you, and you will come to life. Then you will know that I am the LORD.'" So I prophesied as I was commanded. And as I was prophesying, there was a noise, a rattling sound, and the bones came together, bone to bone. I looked, and tendons and flesh appeared on them and skin covered them, but there was no breath in them. Then he said to me, "Prophesy to the breath; prophesy, son of man, and say to it, 'This is what the Sovereign LORD says: Come, breath, from the four winds and breathe into these slain, that they may live.'" So I prophesied as he commanded me, and breath entered them; they came to life and stood up on their feet—a vast army. Then he said to me: "Son of man, these bones are the people of Israel. They say, 'Our bones are dried up and our hope is gone; we are cut off.' Therefore prophesy and say to them: 'This is what the Sovereign LORD says: My people, I am going to open your graves and bring you up from them; I will bring you back to the land of Israel. Then you, my people, will know that I am the LORD, when I open your graves and bring you up from them. I will put my Spirit in you and you will live, and I will settle you in your own land. Then you will know that I the LORD have spoken, and I have done it, declares the LORD'" (Ezekiel 37:1-14).

Ezekiel received a powerful vision from the Lord. This vision, filled with vivid imagery, speaks of the restoration of Israel. He is promising them, though they are hopeless and exiled, that they will be restored to the nation of Israel.

When looking for important details in a passage, I always teach my students to look for repeated words. In this passage of scripture, bones are referred to quite often, so they must be important. With such symbolism in this passage, I'm sure we all could come up with multiple symbols for bones. However, one meaning that stood out to me was that bones are our innermost, what holds our flesh together.

Often my bones, my innermost, feel like Israel's at this time: "Our bones are dried up and our hope is gone; we are cut off" (v. 11). My bones (innermost) often feel dried up, overwhelmed, anxious, distracted, tired, worthless and on and on and on!! Sometimes, even the daily responsibilities of life can make me lose hope and feel despair.

Thankfully, just as the Lord gave a powerful promise to Israel, He has given us the same promise. Just like Israel, He will **awaken** us with the **power** of *His Spirit* so that our dried up bones will **stand strong** on our feet (v. 10). He will put *His Spirit* in us and we will **live** (v. 14). The **living, strong, powerful** *Spirit of God* is in us! May our **hope** overflow as we remember His promises and ask *His Spirit* to fill our lives.

-Melissa Larios

"For God has not given us a spirit of fear,
but of power and of love and discipline" (2 Timothy 1:7).

I have a wonderful life…I am living life as a blessed lady! However, when I was diagnosed with a health condition a few years ago, it spiraled me into six- weeks of anxiety. I had never experienced such a thing in all of my life! The Lord pulled me out of it quickly and set my feet on firm ground. He visited me in the night hours and commanded me not to be afraid. He also showed me that He was using this 'thorn in my flesh' for His glory and to draw me closer to Him. I was reminded to take one day at a time, for this is His will. I learned the importance of taking my thoughts captive and putting into practice that *God has not given me a spirit of fear, but of power, and love and self-discipline* (2 Tim. 1:7) and another great verse *think it not strange, count it all joy* (1 Peter 4).

There are times I feel completely healed and praise Him for it. If He chooses not to heal me, He will give me the patience and strength that I need to endure it. It's a win/win! I know He has entrusted this to me in His perfect will. I love the quote by Hudson Taylor: "All our difficulties are only platforms for the manifestation of His grace, power, and love".

I have always wondered why the Lord has given so much to me, to all of us. The Lord has brought this verse to mind over and over again 'For everyone to whom much is given, from him much will be required" (Luke 12:48b). He requires me to be obedient, He requires me to trust Him and His Word, He requires me to love others with His love. I have a new understanding that He requires me to trust Him with whatever He sends my way, for His ways are far above my ways and His thoughts above my thoughts (Isaiah 55:9).

What is your 'thorn in the flesh'? Whatever it is, the Lord desires to do a good work in you through it. Be a good solider. Trust Him in the uncertain times. He who began a good work in you, will be faithful to complete it!

-Sheila Walker

"That He would grant you, according to the riches of His glory, to be strengthened with might through His Spirit in the inner man, that Christ may dwell in your hearts through faith; that you, being rooted and grounded in love, may be able to comprehend with all the saints what is the width and length and depth and height— to know the love of Christ which passes knowledge; that you may be filled with all the fullness of God" (Ephesians 3:16-19).

This is a prayer that I need desperately for my own soul and for many others whom I love dearly. Have you ever woken up and thought, "That's not today, is it? Can I not do today? I can't smile and pretend I'm ok any longer, not with them, not there." How is it that we as believers can come to this point of desiring isolation (Proverbs 18:1) when God's unsearchable riches are fully available to me daily, even moment by moment?

My inner man is often hidden beneath the façade of what I want people to see, sometimes even to the point of believing my own delusion. Apart from God's strengthening work on my inner man, there is no hope, I will remain stagnant and unchanged because I lack the resources for change. Yet I must remember all that Christ has given to me through His completed work on the cross. His sacrifice was not to elevate me from my circumstances, but to cause me to realize His abundant love - displayed by the cross - in my circumstances. If I could truly comprehend His love, with all the body of Christ, I would have no need to compensate on the outside for my lack on the inside. Certainly there would be absolutely no lack at all. Knowing Christ to the full means our constant return to the source, so that He can define what is real and not just what we feel. Christ is all-satisfying because He is all we need in every season whether difficult or pleasant.

May this be our prayer for our families, our churches, and ourselves. Remembering who our God is... "Now to Him who is able to do exceedingly abundantly above all that we ask or think, according to the power that works in us, to Him be glory in the church by Christ Jesus to all generations, forever and ever. Amen." (Ephesians 3:20–21)

-Dianna Kottman, Missionary in Leatherhead, England

The Lord really spoke to me one day as I was listening to worship music while cleaning house. The song "Forever Reign" by Hillsong came on. I sang along but had to stop myself after I sang the words "The riches of Your love will always be enough". Sadly, I felt that, as fickle as I am, the riches of God's love are not always enough for me. As I pondered this sobering thought, God in His love reminded me that it's not based on my feelings but upon His truth. His love <u>will</u> always be enough. We are so blessed to be daughters of the King and to be enveloped by His love everyday, even those days when we just aren't "feeling" it's enough.

We have His word as a promise..."Yes, I have loved you with an everlasting love; therefore with loving kindness I have drawn you" (Jeremiah 31:3).

-Diana Harding, Missionary in Porto, Portugal

"Don't let your adornment be merely outward." "Rather let it be the hidden person of the heart, with the incorruptible beauty of a gentle and quiet spirit" (1 Peter 3:3,4).

It is not the outward beauty that is the most important! The outward beauty should not be what I 'wow' people with, but the inward beauty needs to be the most important and that is what should 'wow' people. God doesn't care how beautiful I am or what expensive clothing I wear. Of course this doesn't mean for me not to wear nice clothing, or not to be well kept, it's just that these things aren't the most important to God.

When I first read these verses about being gentle & quiet, I figured it would be easy for me to keep these because I am naturally shy and I am not very talkative. Yet God is not speaking of a mute person here, but a <u>heart</u> that is gentle and quiet. When I actually figured out the meaning of the words "gentle and quiet" I realized I have a lot to improve on. Gentle means being humble and quietly following God's desire. Quiet means having the fear of the Lord, and trusting in God.

Gentleness is quite difficult to produce in my life and I can't do it on my own. God is the only one that can do this work in me. A fruit of the Spirit is "gentleness", and so the Holy Spirit can help me grow in gentleness and quietness, because God is concerned about the hidden person of the heart.

1 Peter 3:4 is my favorite verse because I desire to have this incorruptible beauty of a gentle and quiet spirit. I would like for this beauty to work in me because it is incorruptible or as in Hungarian it "never fades." "This is valuable to God!"

-Izabella Ampe, Missionary in Sopron, Hungary

Down and Out, What Now?

"But be doers of the Word, and not hearers only,
deceiving yourselves" (James 1:22).

We are a missionary family We travel a lot by any mode of transport that is available at the moment. We happened to be in Kiev, Ukraine at the train station en route to the airport. We had stopped for a bite to eat. Then, I heard and saw something peculiar. Squish, squish, cruuuuunch, crackled the two former water bottles now turned into recycled shoes. Many of us tried not to stare at his shoes but it caught the attention of many passerby coming and going. Just like many others, I tried not to glance too long at this ingenious man's dirt laden, filthy feet. I couldn't help myself. He had taken water bottles, crushed them, tied them with some twine and "whaaa-lla", there were two homemade water bottle shoes. It cost him nothing but his imagination!

Yet I cringed. Here at the train station, it seemed as if my conscious were caught between two extremes. On one hand, I had seen homeless men and women living on the streets for years. I have met all kind of down-and-out-people. My thoughts always came back to the same revolving door. Why are you here? Was it a fault of your own, drugs, alcohol? Was it no fault of your own? Did he loose his job, his apt., his wife, his kids? As I said a quick prayer for him, my glance turned elsewhere. My kids and luggage were across the street, I needed to herd them onto a bus to be whisked off in an airplane to the other side of the world. I knew that I would be comfortable on the airplane; I would be hugging my family and friends on the other end. I knew that the people who raised me would be welcoming me back home with open arms. My thoughts vacillated from one extreme to another: sheer poverty to wealth.

Yet, with all of the experience I have had with homeless people, I wanted to do more than pray. My first response was to give the man my shoes. I felt for him. Yet, I was still contemplating the fact that he had made himself recycled shoes and although probably not too comfortable, they were practical in his current bind. It was almost ingenious! Bam! The epiphany hit me like a lead weight! If I were living out the Good Samaritan story...who would I be like? I can be like one of three men, the temple helper, the priest (who, by the way, never helped at all) or the Samaritan who bandaged the man's cuts and paid for his stay at the inn.

In some situations, I may only be available to pray. In other circumstances, I might be able to stop and help someone. Do you know someone who has been laid off, recently evicted, lost their home, been given grave news about a loved one? What can you or I do today to help someone in need? Let's first start on our knees!

-Janette Carter, Missionary in Vinnytsia, Ukraine

"This is love: not that we loved God, but that He loved us and sent His Son as an atoning sacrifice for our sins" (I John 4:10).

So you're just not good enough? Too many dark secrets? Christ knows and sees them all, and loves you still. You may have been abandoned, even abused, but His love is deeper still. Jesus will never leave you His compassion for you is everlasting. The Creator of the universe created you, died for you, loves you! He longs for intimate fellowship with you.

"Behold what manner of love the Father has bestowed on us, that we should be called children of God!"
I John 3:1

If you haven't yet… say "yes" to Jesus! He is the peace you long for. He is the love you've always needed!

-Laura Hales

"And do not present your members as instruments of unrighteousness to sin, but present yourselves to God as being alive from the dead, and your members as instruments of righteousness to God" (Romans 6:13).

If you're like me, you may have had an invisible checkbox next to this verse. Most of us, at some time or another, have seen this verse and thought "members" pertained to...let's say...unmentionable parts. We've likened these "members" primarily to sexual intimacy. Logically then, you think to yourself, 'Whew! I'm not fornicating, nor am I committing adultery!', so the box gets the proverbial mental check mark, and we move on to the next verse. Thank you Jesus! Next!

But, in prayer, and in His presence recently, I have seen this verse in a new light. How do we normally see? Most of us process the world around us through our five senses. I wonder if the Lord is commissioning a daily rededication of our "members": Our eyes, to see His face clearly through the world, our ears, to hear His still, small voice louder than the noise, our hands, to touch, like the Good Samaritan, the one everyone else passes by, our nose, to remind us to be a sweet smelling aroma to our God through our actions, and finally, our mouths, surrendering wholly to Jesus and allowing our words to bring only encouragement and life.

As you pray day by day, try telling Jesus this new game plan for your members. Present them to Him as an offering. Let's pray every day, until surrender becomes our habit, until submission becomes our ordinary, and until we're changed from glory to glory.

Until we see Him face to face,

Audra Moraga

Cast thy burden upon the LORD, and He shall sustain thee;
He shall never suffer the righteous to be moved" (Psalm 55:22).

Let me start with this confession. I, Claire Aleman, am a recovering burden hoarder. Yes, it is true. As a child, I thought this verse sounded easy. Why wouldn't you give God your burdens? What I didn't realize then, and what my husband graciously tells me quite often now, is that I take on too much. I have six kids, so it is hard to argue with him as I do have a heavy load on my back. So, why am I not the first in line to hand these cares and worries over to a very willing, very able, loving God?

Perhaps it's because the burden weighing me down the most is having children with special needs. As their mother, I feel solely responsible for their rehabilitation. Not only do I feel I need to carry their burdens, but I feel the need to carry my own. I was taking a walk with a friend when the topic of a television show we had both seen came up. The topic was about people addicted to collecting things. Hoarders. We discussed how crazy it seemed these people wouldn't take the help they were being offered. It seemed so ridiculously simple – "You, Mr. Hoarder, have a house full of trash literally up to your ears, and we're here to clean it up and carry it away for free. Why are you saying no?"

Suddenly it clicked. I stopped dead in my tracks and exclaimed, "I am a burden hoarder!" Jesus has knocked on the door of my heart, and I invited Him in. Now He wants to clean my heart, and carry away all the burdens, but I say, "No." I picture the Lord sitting in my heart amongst all the anger, all the hurt, and all the burdens I refuse to hand over piled up like trash. He looks at me and says, "can I take this for you?" When He holds up some old resentment I have been storing, I say, "No. That's mine. I might need it someday." He holds up another one. "What about this one, Claire? May I please take this off your hands, child?" I reply, "Lord, I can't. All of this is just too important to me, and I can't part with it now. Let's just leave everything as is." He goes back to the only clean area in the room and sits closed in amongst all the filth. Because of my unwillingness, He cannot move in my life. The lack of space leaves room for little else. Where do I store the blessings? The hope? I need to make room. I have to be honest that the clean-up is a daily process. There are weeks where I can feel the clutter returning, and I have to picture my Savior beckoning me to let Him help. I just need to ask.

Take a good look at your heart. Maybe yours is not as messy as mine. Perhaps you are a more organized burden hoarder. Maybe all of your cares and worries are filed neatly away in filing cabinets or storage containers. However you look at it, they are taking up very valuable square footage. I know the One who is more than willing to take them off your hands.

-Claire Aleman

"But without faith *it is* impossible to please *Him,* for he who comes to God must believe that He is, and *that* He is a rewarder of those who diligently seek Him" (Hebrews 11:6).

Living by "faith" can sometimes be so very hard, because as the scripture also says...Now faith is the substance of things hoped for, the evidence of things not seen....Hebrews 1:1   That is why it is called "FAITH".

As I walk this path of faith with the Lord, I have learned to take the good circumstances along with the bad.   Sometimes, faith can be in direct opposition to common sense. Many times, I think I know the way God should fix or deal with things, but for some reason, my ways are not His ways. It's the end result of trusting Him that always shows me "His" perfect plan. It is that faith, once tested, that continues to grow and bring forth fruit.

In Matthew 14, when Peter was out on the boat and saw Christ walking on the water, he became afraid. Christ said, "come". Peter got out of the boat and walked on water to Jesus. When he saw the wind and the churning waters around him, he began to sink.   He cried "Lord, save me!" Immediately Jesus reached out his hand and caught him, "you of little faith, why did you doubt?" In this life, I have learned, or I am learning, to keep my eyes fixed on Jesus. If I take them off of Him for even a second, I begin to sink. My faith is made strong by hiding His promises in my heart. I rely on those promises when I am weak and feel that there is no hope.
When the "Potter" is working with clay, sometimes he has to squish the clay down and remold it into the vessel that he desires. In the end, it ends up the vessel that He intends it to be.

It is trusting Him wholly, giving Him every circumstance, knowing that He who began a good work in me, will be faithful to complete it...Phil 1:6 It is that faith that is hoped for, not seen that allows me to grow in my trust of my Heavenly Father. I only need to give it to Him and put my faith and trust in Him.

One of my mother's favorite poems says it all:

Reproof

As children bring their broken toys with tears for us to mend,
I took my broken dreams to God, because He is my friend.
But instead of leaving Him in peace, to work alone,
I hung around and tried to help with ways that were my own.
At last I snatched them back and cried, "How could you be so slow"
"My child", He said, "What could I do?......
You never did let go."
Author: Unknown

-Laurie Lusk

God's Word, God's Promises, God's Faithfulness
"For Nothing is Impossible with God" (Luke 1:37).

My husband Bob and I have been married for 33 years . We were married April 26,1980, in Lake Tahoe, California.. In October of 1993, I asked Jesus into my heart to help me with some difficult things that were going on in my life. God was faithful. As I shared all of my hurts and poured out my heart to Him, He immediately poured out His love and forgiveness upon me. It felt like I was sitting at the bottom of Niagara Falls and God kept washing over me with His cleansing water. I didn't know what it was at the time but later when I told my friend Lori, (who led me to the Lord on that wonderful day in October), she said that it was the Holy Spirit. I fell in love with God that day and I knew I wanted to follow Him the rest of my life.

As time went on and I learned more about the Lord, I knew I wanted my husband and best friend, Bob, to know my great God for himself. I knew it would be an uphill battle because my husband professed to be an atheist and didn't want anything to do with God. I began to read Gods promises from the Bible. There were so many good ones that I clung to. One of my favorite verses is 2 Peter 3:9: "The Lord is not slack concerning His promise, as some count slackness, but is long suffering toward us, not willing that any should perish but that all should come to repentance."

My husband's salvation became one of the main purposes in my life. I prayed all the time for him to know the peace of Jesus. I asked just about every Christian I knew if they would also pray for Bob.   It was a long journey and I felt beat down many times and would get so discouraged when Bob would put me down for my faith. But, God is faithful........

On September 15th, 2012, my husband, Bob, who had suffered from terrible bouts of anxiety over our many years of marriage, came to the end of trying to deal with it himself. After praying for his salvation for 19 years, on that glorious day, he asked Jesus to come into his heart and to help him. He now knows that great and wonderful God that I know and now we get to share the fullness of our precious Jesus together. God is Faithful. Amen!

-Judy Hahn

"Be anxious for nothing, but in everything by prayer and
supplication, with thanksgiving,
Let your requests be made known to God; and the peace of God,
which surpasses all understanding, will guard your hearts and
minds through Christ Jesus" (Philippians 4:6-7).

I am an anxious person by nature. I take my concerns (and the
concerns of others), and think about them, worry about them, and
ponder them in my mind. This takes my focus and puts it on me
and the problem instead of putting my focus on Jesus. He tells us
not to worry or be anxious and then tells us how to do that. He
wants us to lift everything up to Him in prayer and put all our
concerns in His hands, then remember to thank Him for who He is
and the many ways He blesses us. As we do this He gives us His
peace which will guard our hearts and minds in Christ Jesus.

I invite you to join me in praising our loving God, thanking Him for
His goodness toward us, and lay all our burdens at His feet. For His
Word says to *cast all your care upon Him, for He cares for you.* (1 Peter
5:7).

-Jennifer Glenn

"Whenever I am afraid, I will trust You" (Psalm 56:3).

Some years ago I found myself in one of those difficult places we come to in this journey of life. Having undergone an unsuccessful and distressing heart procedure, I was now facing another one. However, this time I would be traveling to the Mayo Clinic for a 12 hour procedure. Weeks before the appointment I made many phone calls to the hospital and the insurance company trying to get answers to my two main questions regarding the likelihood of success and insurance coverage. I was getting no answers and one day I hung up the phone after another frustrating call when I heard that still small voice whispering to me, 'do you trust Me?' In that instant I knew that question had nothing to do with my concerns but the Lord was asking me if I trusted Him with my very life. He brought to the surface the fear I had been ignoring through keeping busy. At that moment I had a choice. I bowed my head before Him and said, yes, I trust you Lord. Peace filled me as I knew that my life was in His faithful hands.

That question lingers today every time one of His children faces a fearful situation. Will we trust Him? In those deep valleys when that is hard to do, pick up the Word of God for we know that faith comes by hearing and hearing by the Word of God. As you read, let the truth of who He is saturate your soul. He is faithful. He loves you and He will never leave you nor forsake you. Also, follow the Psalmists example in Psalm 77:11 when he says, 'I will remember the works of the Lord.' Recounting all that He has already done for you in the past helps you to realize He is here for you now as that present help in your time of need.

In my trial, the Lord amazingly intervened, redirecting my path to a new local doctor. My appointment at the Mayo Clinic was canceled. It ended up taking three more procedures, locally, but my complex arrhythmia was fixed which I thank and praise the Lord for continually!

So with whatever troubling circumstance that brings anxiety or fear, be it small or large, let us turn to our faithful Lord, to His Word and remember all He's done for us so that we can join the Psalmist and say, 'Whenever I am afraid, I will trust in You.'

-Heidi Brown

"Looking unto the promise of God, he staggered not at the promise
of God through unbelief; but was strong in faith, giving glory to
God, and being fully persuaded that what He had promised He was
able also to perform"
(Romans 4:20-21).

For the past three years or so, my faith has been challenged. During
this time, God has shown me how much I depend on seeing to
believe. It's so much easier to trust God when the steps He is
working are obvious or tangible. It is so much harder when there is
no evidence that my prayers are being answered, or maybe even
heard.

We know that we serve a God of compassion, grace and love. He is
ever faithful to His Word and His promises, as He proves to us over
and over. We have only to look back to see how God has made
provision or miraculously provided for us. One of the things God
has shown my in this three-year journey is that when I let vain
imaginations run rampant in my mind is when my faith is at its
weakest, doubting what God has shown me. When I can't see what
God is doing, I imagine all the reasons why what I want God to
accomplish is not being done.

What I am learning is to focus on God, Himself, and not on what I
want or expect Him to do. Read His Word, pray, fellowship; these
things all help to grow our faith and give us a right picture of who
God is. As we see Him as He is, our faith grows and we become
able to trust that what He has for us is what is best for us. We can
trust that He is for us, and His plans for us are perfect.

-Jackie Fountain

Jr. High
&
High School

"Have I not commanded you? Be strong and courageous. Do not be terrified or discouraged, for the Lord your God will be with you wherever you go" (John 1:9).

John 1:9 is special to me because when I had nightmares, my mom gave me this verse to feel better. It helps me to remember that God is with me. It's comforting because no matter where I go, or what circumstances I face, the Lord is with me and will give me strength.

-Cailey Martin, Jr. High

This hope we have as an anchor of the soul,
both sure and steadfast" (Hebrews 6:19a).

What this verse means to me is that God is our hope and anchor and that if we are in Him, the storms of this world can't move us. He is our protector and will keep us from drifting away. Knowing this makes me have more trust in God – He will always be there for me.

-Sydney Caggegi, Junior High

"Pure and undefiled religion before God and the Father is this: to visit orphans and widows in their trouble, and to keep oneself unspotted from the world" (James 1:27).

This verse means to look after people who aren't as fortunate as we are and to help them when they get distressed.

-Malia Patopoff, Junior High

"I was glad when they said to me,
'let us go to the house of the Lord" (Psalm 122:1).

This verse refreshes me from sin and things that I have done that the Lord is not pleased with. This verse lets me know that someday I will really be in the house of the Lord, even though I do things wrong; He forgives me and helps me through life.

~Rebekah Hensley, Junior High

With man this is impossible, but with God,
all things are possible" (Matthew 19:26)

A lot of people say it is impossible to do a lot of things and I believe them. I say often that I can't do something or that it's impossible, until I remember this verse. It helps me to know that I can do things with God that I can't with man. It helps me to get close to the Lord.

-Eden Aleman, Junior High

"Rejoice in our confident hope, be patient in trouble,
and keep praying" (Romans 17:17).

This verse has really helped me get through a lot of really hard
times. It helps me to be patient and to always pray. It also
helped me realize that sometimes all you can do is pray and
when you pray, the Lord will listen to you and help you!

-Hailey Perez, Junior High

"Yea, though I walk through the valley of the shadow of
death, I will fear no evil;
Your rod and Your staff they comfort me" (Psalm 23:4).

When I was a little girl, I was always afraid of everything,
even though I knew the Lord. My mom helped me by reading
me this verse. It just struck my heart and then I knew the
Lord was with me so I wasn't afraid anymore.

-Grace Colunga, Junior High

The Story of Easter

Easter is a time of family and friends when Jesus saved us so we can start all over again. He died on the cross just for us without Him we would have no luck. He never made a mistake, he was always right and lived a perfect life. He carried the cross on His back and He did it just like that. He wore the crown of thorns. They tore His clothes. He was nailed to the cross that very day, which was sad to see in any way. They yelled foolish things at Him, and yes He could have said "Father stop this instant, I am an innocent man, I have done nothing wrong, why am I hanging on a cross?" He did not say anything, nothing at all, until the very end when He said it all, "It is finished, Father I give you my life", and right there let Himself die.

Now I think we all know the very end, it's when Christ our Savior rose again! He hung on the cross in our place, so let's thank Him and give him all praise!

-Malia Patopoff, Junior High

"I can do everything through Him who gives me strength"
(Philippians 4:13).

When Mrs. Lupe read this verse in front of all of the girls, I thought that it was true that the Lord gives me strength through everything I do. This verse means that when I'm in school, working on math and I feel like I can't do it, with His strength, I know I can.

-Audrey Garcia, Junior High

"Four things on earth are small, yet they are extremely wise: Ants are creatures of little strength, yet they store up their food in the summer, hyraxes are creatures of little power, yet they make their home in the crags; locusts have no king, yet they advance together in ranks;
a lizard can be caught with the hand, yet it is found in kings' palaces" (Proverbs 30:24-28).

As you have read, this verse states that small things can overcome and amaze the bigger, more powerful things. Think of yourself a teenager at school, you may be smaller and more unpopular than others. You notice that the popular girls have designer clothes, expensive makeup and of course, money. All you may have is a worn t-shirt, old sweater, blue jeans and used-to-be white sneakers. Yet some of the 'popular girls' may become jealous of you and may spread gossip and try to hurt you. You are called to a higher calling, answer in love.

But you do have something some of them don't have...a relationship with God. You don't need fancy clothes, heel-pinching shoes, or a boyfriend (that can wait a while), tell others about God! You might become more popular for the right things!

-Marissa Burell, High School

Also...add to your faith...-2 Peter 1:5. In the matter of drudgery. Peter said in this passage that we have become "partakers of the divine nature" and that we should now be "giving all diligence," concentrating on forming godly habits (2 Peter 1:4-5). We are to "add" to our lives all that character means. No one is born either naturally or supernaturally with character; it must be developed. Nor are we born with habits— we have to form godly habits on the basis of the new life God has placed within us. We are not meant to be seen as God's perfect, bright-shining examples, but to be seen as the everyday essence of ordinary life exhibiting the miracle of His grace. Drudgery is the test of genuine character. The greatest hindrance in our spiritual life is that we will only look for big things to do. Yet, "Jesus . . . took a towel and . . . began to wash the disciples' feet . . ." (John 13:3-5).

We all have those times when there are no flashes of light and no apparent thrill to life, where we experience nothing but the daily routine with its common everyday tasks. The routine of life is actually God's way of saving us between our times of great inspiration which come from Him. Don't always expect God to give you His thrilling moments, but learn to live in those common times of the drudgery of life by the power of God.

It is difficult for us to do the "adding" that Peter mentioned here. We say we do not expect God to take us to heaven on flowery beds of ease, and yet we act as if we do! I must realize that my obedience even in the smallest detail of life has all of the omnipotent power of the grace of God behind it. If I will do my duty, not for duty's sake but because I believe God is engineering my circumstances, then at the very point of my obedience all of the magnificent grace of God is mine through the glorious atonement by the Cross of Christ.

-Oswald Chambers, *My Utmost for His Highest*

"If I ask to be delivered from trial rather than for deliverance out of it,

to the praise of His glory;

if I forget that the way of the cross leads to the cross and not to a bank of flowers;

if I regulate my life on these lines,

or even unconsciously my thinking,

so that I am surprised when the way is rough and think it strange,

though the word is,

"Think it not strange,"

"Count it all joy,"

then I know nothing of Calvary love".

-Amy Carmichael

If: What Do I Know of Calvary Love by Amy Carmichael, © 1938 by the Dohnavur Fellowship. Used by permission of CLC Publications. May not be further reproduced. All rights reserved.

TIME ALONE WITH JESUS

JESUS OFTEN WITHDREW TO LONELY PLACES AND PRAYED.

Luke 5:16, **NIV**

Often when I am under stress and pressure, I feel one of my greatest needs is to get a good night's sleep. But I've found that physical rest alone is not enough to revive my flagging spirit. I need the spiritual revival that comes from spending quiet time alone with Jesus in prayer and in thoughtful meditation on His Word.

A careful study of the life of Jesus reveals that as pressed as He was, He "often withdrew to lonely places and prayed." If Jesus felt He needed time alone in prayer with His Father, why do you and I think we can get by without it? How is your prayer life? Could some of the exhaustion you are feeling be the result of simple prayerlessness? How motivating it has been for me to view my early morning devotions as times of retreat alone with Jesus, who desires that I "come with Him by myself to a quiet place" in order to pray, read His Word, listen for His voice, and be renewed in my spirit.

~Anne Graham Lotz

Poetry

"Love of the Cross"

To love those who are hurting
Is an easy thing to do
To love those who love you
Takes no bridled attitude

To love those who have worldly goods
May take a spot of care
To love those who have used you
Will cause your flesh to tear

To love all those who hate you
Will bring you to your knees
For this is not a love that comes
Easy as you please

And loving those befriended
Who cheated you and lied
Will bring you all at once unto
The humble Savior's side

For love is not of fallen man
Who winces with each loss
Love is only found in those
Who glory in the Cross

-Cindy Blackamore

You alone know me.
The deepest part of my being.
My desires, my longing, my hopes   and sorrows.
but the world has been shaping me too far from You and Your love.
Lost and hopeless walking in darkness and loneliness,
far from what I have been created for-- to know my Creator.

But one day,
You came knocking in my broken heart and murmured on my ears
something new,
something from the heaven,
something strange for the world,
something that my heart was longing for since I was born.
Oh Lord who is like You?
Please help me to receive it,
help me to put my hope in it…in You alone!

-Susan Barari-Manzur

"The Warrior"

Storming through the prison door
This warrior does go
Not caring of the time involved
But battling the foe

Living only for one purpose
To regain what has been lost
For the enemy is mighty
And this soldier knows the cost

This warrior has been seasoned
And knows not to get involved
In the cares of temporal living
Upon which this world revolves

This warrior has a mission
Given from the Lord Himself
And seeks with all to fill it
Using wisdom, time and wealth

For nothing is more precious
To this warrior than the call
And experience is telling
That distractions make you fall

The enemy is trembling
At the sound of this advance
He knows against that armor
That he doesn't stand a chance

So look not on the outside
Of the lady that you see
She's small but she is mighty
For she prays on bended knee

-Cindy Blackamore

I decided to go sit in my patio.
Perhaps He will come to meet me there.
As soon as my decision is made, He is there.
I can feel His Spirit moving in the silence
between the fragile branches of white jasmine.
So faithful, so gentle,
in a world of useless rush and harshness,
in a world of hurting and sorrow,
He is my calm, my peace, my joy,
my heaven.
The breeze is touching me gently.
He is the loving touch that I've never known.

-Susan Barari-Manzur

If…

If I take offense easily;

if I am content to continue in a cool unfriendliness,

though friendship be possible,

then I know nothing of Calvary love.

-Amy Carmichael

Spending Time with God

O GOD, YOU ARE MY GOD; EARLY WILL I SEEK YOU; MY
SOUL THIRSTS FOR YOU

(PSALM 63:1).

God seemed to come to my door one day and ask if I would start walking with Him by getting up early in the morning for prayer and Bible reading. At first I thought it was something I had to do. I dragged my feet because I found I didn't want to sacrifice the extra few minutes of sleep! He was so patient as He waited for me to understand that it wasn't something I had to do; instead it was a personal time of fellowship where I could just grow in my love relationship with Him.

One reason I have maintained my walk with God is that no one else - not my beloved family or my close and loyal friends - really understands me. No one else truly knows my fears and longings and hurts and dreams and failures. But He shares my feelings, my loneliness. Spending time with God as I "walk" with Him meets needs that are in the deepest part of me. He Himself is the solution to the loneliness of the human spirit.

-Anne Graham Lotz

Living Simply — Yet Focused

Look at the birds of the air . . . . Consider the lilies of the field . . . —
Matthew 6:26, 28

Consider the lilies of the field, how they grow: they neither toil nor spin" — they simply are! Think of the sea, the air, the sun, the stars, and the moon— all of these simply ARE as well— yet what a ministry and service they render on our behalf! So often we impair God's designed influence, which He desires to exhibit through us, because of our own conscious efforts to be consistent and useful. Jesus said there is only one way to develop and grow spiritually, and that is through focusing and concentrating on God. In essence, Jesus was saying, "Do not worry about being of use to others; simply believe on Me." In other words, pay attention to the Source, and out of you "will flow rivers of living water" (John 7:38). We cannot discover the source of our natural life through common sense and reasoning, and Jesus is teaching here that growth in our spiritual life comes not from focusing directly on it, but from concentrating on our Father in heaven. Our heavenly Father knows our circumstances, and if we will stay focused on Him, instead of our circumstances, we will grow spiritually— just as "the lilies of the field."

The people who influence us the most are not those who detain us with their continual talk, but those who live their lives like the stars in the sky and "the lilies of the field"— simply and unaffectedly. Those are the lives that mold and shape us.

If you want to be of use to God, maintain the proper relationship with Jesus Christ by staying focused on Him, and He will make use of you every minute you live— yet you will be unaware, on the conscious level of your life, that you are being used of Him.

-Oswald Chambers